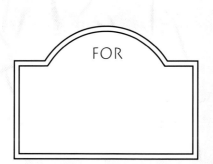

FOR

 Peter Pauper Press, Inc.
White Plains, New York

Conceived by S. M. Skolnick
Copyright ©1997
Peter Pauper Press, Inc.
202 Mamaroneck Avenue
White Plains, NY 10601
All rights reserved
ISBN 0-88088-064-3
Printed in China
7 6 5 4 3 2 1

INTRODUCTION

What is in your hands is not a scholarly work or an intellectualized description of Zen.

—

It is a companion piece that provides the taste of a few dishes from the banquet of life.

—

It is a conversation. It is a silence. It is the result of the sifting of numerous texts, commentaries, and teachings through a skein of material stretched across the wide mouth of a funnel, being held in suspension rather than passing through the small end, but at the same time passing through the small end, appearing on pages, scattering, and appearing again in time to disappear.

Enlightenment is not a step-by-step process. The path is non-rational and Zen cannot be described or approached in intellectual terms. It is often a creature of intuition. It requires an emptying of the mind and not thinking, What is Zen? Zen is Zen. What is The Way? The Way is The Way. We come to know that

each thing has its *isness* and each
action its *suchness*.

———

Enlightenment has no gender.
Then why *A Woman's Book of Zen*?
Simple—for all that is the same
between women and men there is
much that is not the same. Some-
times all roads that lead to the same
destination are different. For all the
experiences that are shared, there are
experiences that are subject to intu-
itions and perceptions that are not
shared. For all the symbols that we
may have in common, there are symbols that emerge from this sensibility

or that. Until recently much of the traditions and literature of Zen and Zen life that have been available to the English language reader have been dominated by male figures and male patterns of behavior. Scholars and practitioners like Susan Murcott, Anne Carolyn Klein, and Sylvia Boorstein, among others, have contributed greatly to illuminating the woman's perspective. In its small and portable fashion this book also seeks to do so.

———

The primary motivation for the creation of this work has been inspiration provided by two important books: One is *The First Buddhist Women*, by Susan Murcott, a translation and commentary on the *Therigatha*. The *Therigatha* (the verses or songs of the women elders) survived for six centuries through oral tradition before being codified in the 1st century B.C. The second is *Meeting the Great Bliss Queen*, by Anne Carolyn Klein, a work of historical perspective that explores methods of empowerment available to the modern Western woman through Buddhist philosophy and practice.

*How can you measure
importance?
Which breath that you
draw is unimportant?*

THE ART OF MEDITATION

Take time to meditate, to practice *Zazen*. This can be approached by sitting in what is called the Lotus position. Sit on a small round cushion or a low bench. Place your right foot on the left thigh, and the left foot on the right thigh. Straighten your back, but do not strain, so that the tip of your nose and your navel are in alignment. If at first you find that this position is difficult you may wish to try the Half-Lotus position which requires placing one foot on the opposite thigh while tucking the other foot under its opposite thigh. A further simplification is the Quarter-Lotus position. In the Quarter-Lotus one foot is placed on the calf of the opposite leg and the other leg is tucked under the opposite thigh.

—

After you have found a comfortable way to sit, you must find your breath. Breathe calmly, regularly, and deeply from your diaphragm through your nose. Be mindful of the inhalations and exhalations as

each is a breath. Concentrate on
your breathing, with your eyes
partially open. Meditating in
this way should assist you in not
thinking. Not thinking will allow
the gates to open into that which
is empty.

———

You may wish to consult more
thorough sources and works of practical instruction in sitting, breathing and meditating on the path to
not knowing.

———

Not knowing may also, in
what may seem to be a paradox, be

associated with mindfulness. See each moment as entirely new, come to each moment and each experience with freshness. Do not restrict your mindfulness to formal times of meditation. Be mindful of your skin, and the hair separate from the skin in which it is anchored. Be mindful of your feet apart from your body, your toes apart from your feet. If you are peeling an onion, be mindful of your fingers separate from your hand, of the utensil being held apart from your fingers, of the blade of the instrument that you hold apart from the handle that secures it, of the blade separate from the onion skin, of the skin apart from the fiber that it envelops, of the fiber separate from the water that is held within the fiber of the onion. If peeling the onion causes tears to form, be mindful of the tears separate from your cheek, of the liquid in the tear as separate from the shape that you call a tear. If you are open to seeing then you are open to enlightenment. If you are enlightened everything is new.

STORIES OF THE WAY

In a town on a hillside just down the road from here was the studio of an artist who also had a reputation as a respected teacher of Zen. It was arranged that a young woman would be her student for one month. The student was required to arrive at the studio each morning one-half hour before sunrise. When she arrived her teacher was always seated near an unpainted canvas that had been placed on an easel. The teacher

motioned for the young woman to be
seated on a cushion and observe as
she placed the tip of her brush,
charged with blue paint, at a point
on the canvas one inch from the top.
The teacher drew a stroke that ended
one inch before the bottom of the
canvas. She re-charged her brush
and began at the spot on the canvas
that had been her starting point and
brought the stroke to a stop one inch
from the bottom of the canvas.
The teacher repeated this activity
until mid-morning, at which point
she would leave the room with her
canvas in hand. Returning with a

new canvas she would position it on the easel at precisely the same angle as the previous one. She would charge her brush with blue paint and begin again one inch from the top of the canvas and draw the hairs of the brush to the resting point one inch from the bottom.

———

This activity continued until mid-afternoon, at which point the teacher would leave the room with her canvas in hand. Returning with a new canvas she would position it on the easel at the same angle as the previous one. The teacher would

charge her brush with blue paint
and begin again one inch from the
top of the canvas and draw the hairs
of the brush to the resting point one
inch from the bottom. When the
sun began to take on its evening
color she would put down her brush,
acknowledge her student, and leave
the studio with her canvas in hand.
A few minutes later the student
would leave the studio through an-
other doorway.

———

On her last day under tutelage
the young woman entered the studio, as she had each morning since

her arrival, one-half hour before sunrise. The teacher was sitting in what had been her student's place. Near the easel that had been the teacher's lay a canvas, a brush, and dishes of pigment. The student was precise in positioning the canvas on the easel at the angle that her teacher had consistently favored. She dipped her brush in the pot with the blue paint and placed the pointed hairs of the brush one inch from the top of the canvas. She pulled the stroke down to within one

inch of the bottom and stopped.
She recharged her brush with blue
paint, found the starting place, and
drew the brush down to within one
inch of the bottom of the canvas.
She repeated this activity until mid-
morning when her teacher rose from
the sitting position, removed her
student's canvas from the easel, and
left with it in her hand.

—

The teacher returned to the
studio with open palms. She instructed her student to follow her to
the room where numerous canvases,
each with a multi-layered blue

stroke, were displayed hanging on walls and leaning against wooden boxes. The young woman was overwhelmed at the number of paintings that she saw, but she was most disturbed that she could not distinguish her own painting from the work of others. The teacher, seeing the searching eyes of her student move ever more quickly from canvas to canvas, turned to her and said, "It is clear that you have not yet found your own stroke."

Do not follow an
enlightened one
   but ask her what
she is looking for and
look for it also.

A woman lived in a great tree in a forest of redwoods. This tree towered above the height that we usually associate with trees. The tree's girth far exceeded any one woman's ability to encircle it with her arms and to clasp her right hand with her left. On a clear spring morning a girl carrying a few items of clothing in her pack, and several days' worth of food, stopped to speak with the woman who lived in the tree.

———

The girl asked, "Is this the path

to enlightenment?" "What a magnificent tree this is," the woman replied.

———

"I don't mean to be rude but I am not asking you about the tree. I would like to know if this is the path to enlightenment," retorted the girl.

———

"If you cannot get past the tree, you cannot be on the path," replied the woman.

A young woman would visit with her grandmother each night after the evening meal.

———

The young woman would bring tea and a sweet cake for the older woman to eat while they chatted and she asked her grandmother numerous questions. One evening during the course of a long conversation the lights flickered and went out. The women could see through the window that the street lights had also gone out. The grandmother said that it was just as well that darkness had come as she was tired. She suggested that her granddaughter go downstairs and also retire for the night.

———

"But grandma, I am not accustomed to walking down these stairs in the dark. I could easily trip and fall." "Here is a candle to light your way, granddaughter," she replied.

———

The young woman tightened her hand around the candle and bent over to kiss her grandmother good night. As she did this her grandmother blew out the flame.

What is here with me
is also elsewhere.
What is in my mind is
also in the larger mind.

A woman was very successful in her career, a loving mother to her children, and a supportive and caring mate to her spouse. One morning she found herself feeling that despite the practical accomplishments of many of her activities, her life lacked sufficient meaning. In spite of all that she did each day she felt hollow. She resolved that if she could find more internal strength and renew her energies, the sum of her activities could bring her closer to knowing the meaning of it all.

She had vacation time coming to her at work, knew that her mother would be more than happy to watch her children for a few days, and her spouse would be understanding of her need to take some time for herself.

———

The woman went to a spa recommended to her by a number of her friends. At the spa a simple schedule was arranged, and a thoughtful staff member reminded her of when she needed to be in each place and escorted her to the various facilities. Exercise regimens, massages, facials, wholesome food, and healing baths were arranged. On the morning of the day that she was scheduled to leave the spa a beautifully serene woman sat down across from her in the meditation room. This woman did not speak at first, but made it clear by her posture that the visitor could, if she chose, engage her in conversation or ask questions.

———

"Tell me please why, even though I enjoy my work, adore my children, have love and compassion toward my husband, and have a good self-image, do I feel that something is missing? Is there something that I am doing wrong? Is there something I am not doing? Is there something else that I can do?"

—

"Yes there is," said the woman. "It is not found in pleasures. It is not found in material things. It is not thinking."

Get up and
do nothing.
 Sit here and
do nothing.
 Is the truth
any less clear?

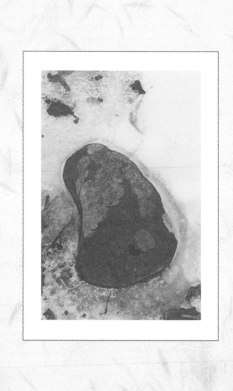

Near a border crossing lived a woman who had built a house for herself using materials that were indigenous to the area. The structure looked so natural in its setting that the casual traveler often did not notice it all. Those few people who did actually see the house admired it but, as they were invariably on their way to somewhere else, they seldom stopped to visit.

A builder had to create a structure that she was required to blend in with its surroundings. The builder was aware of this other woman's house and made arrangements to have her visit the new site. On the day of the woman's arrival, the builder showed her an expansive area that had been dug out to make a place for the laying of the foundation. The builder was full of ideas and spent the whole of the first day talking about how she envisioned this project. The woman and her hostess returned to the site the next day and again the builder went on and on about her philosophy and concepts for the project. When the air around them was heavy with words the woman went into the cab of an earth mover and began pushing the mounded earth at the periphery of the site back into the hole from which it had come. When all the earth had been returned to its place, she began to move material from other piles into the cavity. The builder began waving her hands and shouting frantically to attract the woman's attention, but she did not seem to hear the shouts and kept adding material to the filled-in spot. When all the materials had been mounded on top of what had been the foundation pit, the woman shut down the earth mover and climbed from the cab.

———

At this point, the builder was beside herself. Weeks of work had been reversed. The builder said, "Don't you see that the hole is full; how can I pour a foundation now?"

"Yes," replied the woman, "the hole is no longer a hole. It is filled to overflowing as you are with your own ideas. How can you expect to have space for a foundation if the site is more than filled?"

Empty your mind,
empty the mirror.

"Zen seems so complicated," the taller sister said to the other.

"Will you teach me the way to begin?"

"Have you eaten your lunch?" the shorter one asked.

"Yes," her sister replied.

"Now wash your plate."

The taller girl said to her sister,
"How can I learn enlightenment?
Is there only one way?"

"No," her sister answered,
"Every Way is the Way."

———

"Can I study the Way?" "No,
dear sister, the more that you study
the path to enlightenment the further away the path will take you."

———

"If I am not supposed to study
the Way to enlightenment how will I
know that I have found it?" "The

Way is not a thing to know or not know. You cannot find it in books, on tapes, or on a screen. Open yourself up to nothing, and you will be on the Way."

On a cold spring day a late and sudden snow storm swept across the region. A teacher of Zen found herself unable to return home as the roads were impassable. The teacher was hesitant to ask for additional lodging time at the Bed & Breakfast where she had been staying as she had only enough money for the fare home. The woman who ran the B & B was compassionate by nature and made the teacher feel at ease about staying as long as necessary. Once it was clear that the teacher would stay, the woman engaged her in conversation and confided in her that she had studied Zen for a time but had failed to achieve enlightenment. This frustration had caused her to stop her practice and throw herself with even more vigor into the business of running her inn.

———

The temperature stayed colder than normal for the time of year and the deep snows remained for several days. The innkeeper observed the simplicity of the teacher's movements and the aura of tranquillity that seemed to surround her. After several days the innkeeper felt that she could ask the teacher about her practice and enlist her aid in reapproaching *Zazen* or meditation. The teacher instructed the innkeeper on her posture and breathing and offered her a *koan* or Zen riddle to use.

———

When seasonal temperatures returned they came with the suddenness of the earlier storm. The snow and ice melted quickly, saturating the ground with water and filling the basement of the B & B faster than the pump and drainage system could handle. The innkeeper found it necessary to bail water with buckets to minimize the damage that was being done. A number of guests who were far behind in their schedules moved on as soon as the roads were passable.

———

The teacher, however, who felt that her brief lessons to the owner were not sufficient to repay the kindness she had been shown, offered to help in the clean-up. The women carried buckets of water up out of the basement and emptied them in a nearby pond. This work continued into the evening when the sun had faded away and the moon rose round and bright. The moon reflected in the innkeeper's full bucket. Her body was weary from the work. As she stumbled over a small pile of stones, the handle came loose and the bucket fell and splintered. The water spilled onto the ground and the moon's reflected image disappeared. Regaining her footing, the innkeeper said in an interior voice: "The bucket is broken, the water is on the ground, the moon is no longer in my hand, it is empty."

*If you have nothing in
your mind, throw it out.*

A quilter who wished to pre-
serve the history of her family col-
lected many pieces of cloth from
clothing that had been worn by family members during significant
events in their lives. Over a period
of many years she gathered hun-
dreds of squares from baby blankets,
graduation robes, evening gowns,
wedding dresses, a suit that someone
wore on her first day at a new job,
and many other items of apparel.
The quilter kept the squares in a
room on the top floor of her home

where she spent an equal number of
years piecing the quilt together. One
night a fire broke out in her child's
room. The woman threw the quilt
on the flames and pressed down
hard. The fire was smothered but
the quilt was charred beyond recog-
nition. The quilter swept up the
ashes and scattered them in the
garden.

——

Over the next several years the
quilter again asked each family
member for other bits of cloth so
that she could sew the quilt again. It
took her an equal number of years

to collect the new squares, and piece
a new quilt.

———

East of where this woman lived
several seasons of crops had failed,
and the families who worked the
farmland lost their homes and their
ability to make a livelihood. As the
farmers migrated west, passing
through her town, many of them
didn't even have a blanket to keep
their children warm at night. It is
said that the quilter cut her over-
sized quilt into several smaller
spreads so that they could be used
by those less fortunate travelers to

warm and comfort their children.

—

By the time that she began to collect pieces for the third quilt she was an old woman.

—

Her eyesight was faltering, and her fingers worked the needle with difficulty. But she persevered and gathered the full complement of squares—plus many more since the number of significant events had increased with time. The woman, now very old, died on a starry summer night, passing on with the completed quilt in her hand. The third quilt is now on display in a museum. People who see it are moved beyond emotion at its grandness and beauty. But it is said by those who know that the first two quilts, which have never been seen, far outshone the third.

Do I need to know
the sound of one hand
clapping now that I have
heard the sound of a cloud
passing before the sun?

The "beginner's mind" is an open mind.

There are no experts here.

BIBLIOGRAPHY AND
SUGGESTED READING

Boorstein, Sylvia, *Don't Just Do Something, Sit There: A Mindfulness Retreat with Sylvia Boorstein*. (HarperSan Francisco, San Francisco, CA: 1996)

Enomiya-Lassalle, Hugo M. Compiled and edited by Roland Ropers and Bogdan Snela. Translated from the German by Michelle Bromley, *The Practice of Zen Meditation*. (Thorsons, an imprint of HarperCollins, San Francisco, CA: 1995)

Klein, Anne Carolyn, *Meeting the Great Bliss Queen: Buddhists, Feminists, and the Art of the Self.* (Beacon Press, Boston, MA: 1995)

Murcott, Susan, *The First Buddhist Women*: Translations and Commentary on the Therigatha. (Parallax Press, Berkeley, CA: 1991)

Reps, Paul and Senzaki, Nyogen, *Zen Flesh, Zen Bones.* (Shambala, Boston & London: 1994)

Senzaki, Nyogen and McCandless, Ruth Strout, *Buddhism and Zen.* (North Point Press, San Francisco, CA: 1987)